IMPACT OF TECHNOLOGY IN
HISTORY
AND
ARCHAEOLOGY

Alex Woolf

heinemann
raintree

Edited by James Benefield and Amanda Robbins
Designed by Steve Mead
Original illustrations © Capstone Global Library Ltd 2016
Picture research by Tracy Cummins
Production by Helen McCreath
Originated by Capstone Global Library Ltd
Printed and bound in China by RR Donnelley Asia

19 18 17 16 15
10 9 8 7 6 5 4 3 2 1

Library of Congress Cataloging-in-Publication Data
Cataloging-in-Publication Data is available at the Library of Congress website.

ISBN 978-1-4846-2637-5 (hardcover)
ISBN 978-1-4846-2642-9 (paperback)

This book has been officially leveled by using the F&P Text Level Gradient™ Leveling System.

Acknowledgments
Alamy: Agencja Fotograficzna Caro, 4, ARCTIC IMAGES, 21, Barry Iverson, 27, Keren Su/China Span, 19; AP Photo: Leila Gorchev, 13; Art Resource, N.Y: The Art Archive, 17; Capstone Press: HL Studios, 6, 10; Caracol Archaeological Project: Arlen and Diane Chase, 11; Corbis: Bettmann, 16, Boris Roessler/dpa, 48, Cover Bottom, DK Limited, 45, Jim Sugar, 15, Micro Discovery, 35, Reuters/David Brauchli, 47; Getty Images: AFP, 29, 30, China Photos, 43, DigitalGlobe, 7, JACK GUEZ/AFP, 22, Joe Munroe/The LIFE Images Collection, 8, MAHMOUD ZAYAT/AFP, 5, Munshi Ahmed/Bloomberg, 32, NSF/Science Source, 28; iStockphotos: microgen, Cover Top Left; Science Source: Andrew Brookes, National Physical Laboratory, 36, Pasquale Sorrentino, 27, Philippe Psaila, 49, Skyscan, 18, Tek Image, 25; Shutterstock: Artishok, Design Element, Dragan85, Design Element, fotohunter, Cover Top Right, Krivosheev Vitaly, 9, l i g h t p o e t, 39, nikkytok, Cover Top Middle, style_TTT, Design Element; Thinkstock: JDEstevao, 42.

We would like to thank Professor Michael Dee for his invaluable help in the preparation of this book.

CONTENTS

Some words are shown in bold, **like this**. You can find out what they mean by looking in the glossary.

1 HISTORY'S TECHNOLOGICAL REVOLUTION

History is a constantly evolving subject. We have a picture of the past, based on stories handed down to us as well as preserved physical documents, artifacts, and **human remains**. This picture is constantly being updated and improved thanks to the work of historians and archaeologists. Technology provides them with the tools to carry out this work.

Why should we study the past?

Today's world is the result of many thousands of years of human development. Many of the great advances of the modern world, and also its problems, have their roots in our collective past. Only by understanding that heritage will it ever be really possible for us to appreciate, and improve upon, our present-day world.

⩔ Historians search through old documents for clues to help them shed light on the mysteries of the past.

Primary and secondary sources

We learn about the past by searching for and analyzing **evidence**. The most important kind of evidence is primary sources: original materials from the period the historian is researching. They could be documents, artifacts, or historical sites.

Records produced a long time after an event are known as secondary sources. These are useful, especially if there are no primary sources available. However, they are less trustworthy as evidence because the writers did not witness the events they describe.

Archaeology

Many primary sources are discovered through archaeology (the study of the past through the **excavation** of sites and the analysis of things found there). Traditionally, archaeologists relied on luck or informed guesswork in making their discoveries. When they did find materials, dating them or figuring out what they were or how they were used was hard. Technology has changed this.

How technology has helped

Technology has transformed archaeology. Today, new techniques help archaeologists discover and survey sites as well as date and identify the artifacts and human remains they find. Technology allows archaeologists to see beneath the surface of objects, giving them important clues about how things were made and used.

⌃ Some of the best primary sources lie beneath our feet. Archaeologists dig up human remains and artifacts to learn about how people once lived.

2 FINDING HISTORICAL REMAINS

Before archaeologists can analyze remains, they have to find them. Traditionally, they discovered sites by searching for clues in ancient books and manuscripts, listening to local legends, or accidentally finding artifacts. Today, **aerial** and satellite surveying not only help archaeologists to cover much larger areas in their searches, but they also reveal features that aren't obvious when they are on the ground.

Searching from the air

Buried historical sites create impressions rarely seen in nature on the surface of Earth. These are easier to see from the air.

- Shadow marks: Lumps and bumps on the ground are especially visible when the sun is low in the sky, creating "shadow marks."
- Crop marks: Buried ditches hold more water than surrounding land, and buried walls hold less water. This causes crops to grow better or worse, leading to color differences in the landscape. These are known as crop marks. During a 2001 aerial survey of a Roman fort in Kent, United Kingdom, crop marks were found indicating a previously undetected network of roads and buildings.

⩔ Buried ruins cause the crops above them to grow differently. This causes crop marks—an important clue when searching for archaeological sites.

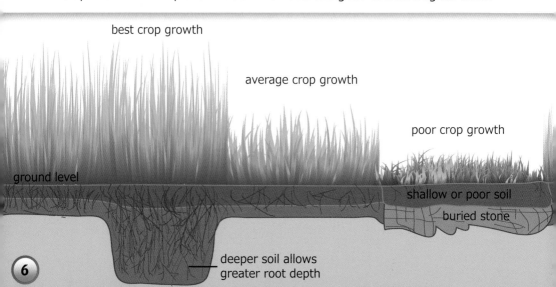

best crop growth

average crop growth

poor crop growth

ground level

shallow or poor soil

buried stone

deeper soil allows greater root depth

- Soil marks: On plowed fields, archaeological remains cause differences in soil color (soil marks).
- Frost marks: On winter fields, water collecting on the lines of buried features can cause frost marks.

Searching from space

Since the 1980s, archaeologists have made use of **high-resolution** satellite photography. Satellites can take photographs using **infrared**. This helps detect wavelengths beyond the visible light spectrum, making it sensitive to color differences in vegetation— ideal for spotting crop marks. Archaeologists used this to research **Mayan** settlements in Guatemala. Satellite photos, taken in 2006, mapped previously unknown roads.

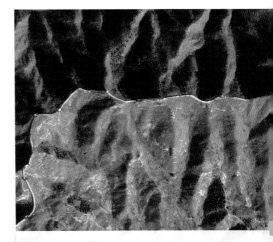

⌃ This satellite photo is of the Great Wall of China. Satellite photography has hugely improved in quality and resolution since it began in the late 1950s.

TECHNOLOGY THROUGH TIME: AERIAL ARCHAEOLOGY

1888: Arthur Batut invents kite photography in France.

1900s: Henry Wellcome, excavating at Jebel Moya, Sudan, sent up kites with cameras attached.

1906: Philip Henry Sharpe of the Royal Engineers' Balloon Section photographs Stonehenge (in the United Kingdom) from a balloon— the first archaeological site to be photographed from the air.

1924: Osbert Guy Stanhope Crawford and Alexander Keiller take photographs of archaeological sites in the United Kingdom from an aircraft. They publish the photos in a book demonstrating to the world the true potential of aerial archaeology.

1930s: Crawford continues to develop aerial archaeology, mapping sites and coining the terms "crop mark" and "soil mark."

Seeing beneath the ground

Today, archaeologists can survey and map a site without even picking up a shovel. They do this with special instruments that can sense structures buried beneath the ground or far below water.

Unearthing with electricity

Electricity does not flow smoothly through all materials. Metals **conduct** electricity, while stone, for example, stops, or resists, the flow. The amount of resistance can be measured using a device called an electrical resistance meter.

These devices detect and map buried archaeological features. For example, a stone foundation might get in the way of the flow of electricity, while a historical dump for domestic waste might conduct it. To measure electrical resistance on a site, archaeologists insert metal probes called electrodes into the ground. Some of these send an electrical current into the earth, while others measure any electrical resistance to it.

Mapping with magnets

It's not just metals such as iron and steel that are magnetic. All materials have their own unique magnetic properties— though some are a lot less magnetic than others. A magnetometer is a highly sensitive device that can pick up magnetic readings from all kinds of materials, several feet underground.

⌃ Magnetometers can be used to survey large sites much more quickly than other devices.

Magnetometers are particularly useful for detecting evidence of burning in ancient human settlements. Burning permanently changes the magnetic properties of soil by altering the magnetism of tiny iron particles contained within it. Ancient hearths, **cremations**, or pits filled with burned materials give strong readings on the magnetometer. Stone wall foundations give a weaker signal.

THE SCIENCE BEHIND: METAL DETECTORS

A metal detector gives a signal whenever it is close to metal, such as old coins or even treasure. But how do metal detectors work? The most common metal detectors consist of a transmitter coil, which sends electric pulses into the ground that interact with any metal objects found there, causing them to create a **magnetic field**. A receiver coil picks up this magnetic field and sends it to a control box to analyze the signal. The control box can calculate the depth of the object based on the signal's strength, and even what kind of metal it is. This is based on how easily electricity passes through it.

⌄ Armed with a metal detector, anyone can be an archaeologist, locating metal objects buried in the ground.

Radar revelations

You might have heard of **radar** before—it's normally used to track aircraft and ships. But when directed at the ground, it can be useful to archaeologists.

Ground-penetrating radar (GPR) sends radio waves into the ground to detect buried objects. When the wave hits an object, the wave bounces back, and a receiving **antenna** records the return signal. The strength of the signal indicates the depth of the object—a stronger signal means the object is closer. GPR can even show the shape of buried features as 3-D images. It is also particularly good at detecting hollow spaces below ground, such as ancient crypts, tombs, mines, or cellars.

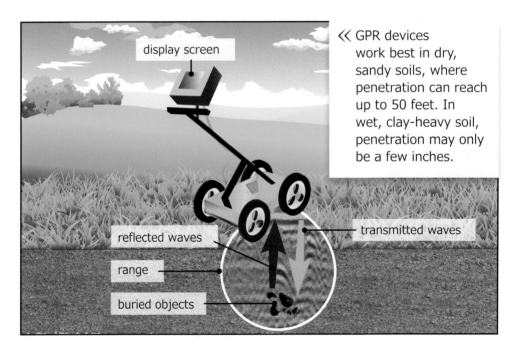

display screen

《 GPR devices work best in dry, sandy soils, where penetration can reach up to 50 feet. In wet, clay-heavy soil, penetration may only be a few inches.

reflected waves

transmitted waves

range

buried objects

Locating with lasers

LIDAR (Laser Imaging Detection and Ranging, or sometimes Light Imaging Detection and Ranging) is a powerful and exciting new tool available to archaeologists. The device, attached to an aircraft, creates amazingly detailed 3-D maps of archaeological sites. It works by transmitting a pulsed laser beam at the ground and then analyzing the reflected light from the beam. A narrow laser beam can map features in great detail, and the use of infrared light enables LIDAR to penetrate clouds, vegetation, and forest canopies.

In 2001, GPR was used to map the northern portion of a site called Lower Market in Petra, Jordan, dating from the **Byzantine** era. Antennae were moved along the ground, transmitting and recording many signals per second. The return signals were plotted to create a 3-D subsurface map of the area to a depth of around 10 feet (3 meters). The map showed a number of interesting buried features, including walls, platforms, and an open area that may have been a garden.

PIONEERS

ARLEN AND DIANE CHASE

In 2010, husband-and-wife archaeology team Arlen and Diane Chase used LIDAR to map a vast complex of ruins at the ancient Mayan city of Caracol, near Belize. They proved the awesome power of LIDAR by collecting more data in 10 hours about the topography (arrangement of physical features) of the site than had been achieved in 30 years of ground-based archaeology. With LIDAR, they mapped 77 square miles (199 square kilometers) of the site; until then, just 7.7 square miles (19.9 square kilometers) had been mapped.

∧ In this 3-D LIDAR image of Caracol, the tree cover has been removed. The agricultural terraces the Maya built to feed their populations are visible as ripples in the hillsides.

Searching for shipwrecks

Marine archaeologists face unique challenges when looking for shipwrecks. The first stage of any shipwreck hunt is not necessarily technological: it involves combing through historical records, such as deck logs, reports, and letters, for clues to the vessel's last known location. Once an approximate location has been pinned down, technology comes into play.

Cameras

The simplest type of search can be done by one or several cameras at the end of a cable towed by a ship. The wreck of the *Titanic* was found using this method in 1985. However, this is a slow process and is very expensive: shipwreck hunts can cost up to $60,000 per day, so archaeologists are always eager to find more efficient search methods.

Sonar

Sonar is a system used for detecting underwater objects by sending out sound waves (which travel efficiently through water) and then analyzing their echoes. Marine archaeologists use a device called a side-scan sonar, which is towed behind the ship or fixed to its **hull**. It sends out fan-shaped pulses of sound toward the sea floor. This creates a picture of the sea floor several hundred yards to either side of the ship.

Side-scan sonar can also distinguish between different materials. For example, the wood or metal of a shipwreck produces a louder echo than the surrounding sand. Side-scan sonar was used in 1967 to explore less accessible parts of the flagship, called *Mary Rose*, of England's King Henry VIII.

Magnetometers at sea

Magnetometers (see pages 8 and 9) are also very useful at sea. A magnetometer towed behind a boat can pick up variations in Earth's magnetic field caused by the presence of metal remains, such as iron hulls and anchors. Unlike cameras or sonar, magnetometers can even pick up readings from wrecks buried beneath the sea floor.

TECHNOLOGY THROUGH TIME: MARINE ARCHAEOLOGY

1836: Charles and John Deane invent the diving helmet and discover the 16th-century wreck of the *Mary Rose*.

1929–1932: The first **systematic** archaeological investigation of a shipwreck: the Nemi Ships (2,000-year-old Roman ships in Lake Nemi) were examined on land after being towed ashore.

1933–1939: The first underwater marine archaeology is carried out by divers on the Swedish 16th-century warship *Elefanten*.

1942–1943: Emile Gagnan and Jacques Cousteau invent the aqualung (a portable breathing apparatus), opening up the underwater world for divers.

1960: George Bass and Peter Throckmorton investigate a 3,200-year-old shipwreck in Turkey, proving that underwater archaeology can be done to the same standards as on land.

1980s: The development of remotely operated underwater vehicles (ROVs) makes it possible to explore deep-water sites.

⌄ Divers raise a statue of a priest from a temple to the Egyptian god Isis. The statue dates from the first century CE. They found it on the submerged island of Antirhodos, off the coast of Egypt.

3 DATING TECHNIQUES

So, you've dug up an artifact. Now, one of the first objectives for any archaeologist is to figure out how old it is.

Before the 20th century, there was no way to date an object in years (known as absolute dating). Archaeologists had to be content with a rough guess of an object's age, based on previous knowledge. They could determine whether an object was older or newer than another object (known as relative dating), using methods such as:

- stratigraphy—older objects tend to be found beneath newer ones
- seriation—finding clues in the style or design of a piece of pottery, for example.

The first absolute dating system for archaeology wasn't developed until 1901, by American scientist Andrew Ellicott Douglass.

THE SCIENCE BEHIND: STRATIGRAPHY

Since the late 19th century, archaeologists have used stratigraphy (the study of soil layers, or "strata") to help them date finds and place them in context with other objects. Objects found in the same layer of soil are from the same period of time. Generally speaking, the deeper the object is buried, the older it is.

Tree time

Douglass discovered that a tree's growth rings (the rings a tree produces each year, which you can see when you cut through a section of a trunk) varied in size depending on the climate, with wider rings in wet years and narrower rings in dry years. He could figure out the age of a piece of wood based on its final growth ring. Douglass called this dating method dendrochronology.

CASE STUDY / THE FAIRBANKS HOUSE

The Fairbanks House in Dedham, Massachusetts, is traditionally regarded as the oldest surviving timber-framed house in North America. According to historical records, it was built around 1640 by Puritan settler Jonathan Fairebanke. In 2001, dendrochronologists decided to test this claim by analyzing some of the building's timber beams. They discovered that the wood was from an oak tree cut down in 1637–1638, confirming the building's age.

Problems with precision

Dendrochronology is by no means a perfect dating method. Although it can reveal the date the tree was cut down and turned into timber, it can't necessarily tell you the age of the object made from that tree—after all, the timbers may have been reused from an earlier structure or artifact. Another problem is that not all timbers include the final growth ring, making the year the tree was cut down difficult to determine. Having said that, dendrochronology—when it works— can be extraordinarily precise: no other dating method gives you the age of an object to the exact year.

⌄ By examining many different trees in a given area, dendrochronologists have been able to create tree-ring chronologies stretching back many thousands of years.

Clues from carbon

Dendrochronology can only date wooden objects. The next breakthrough in dating—radiocarbon dating—enabled archaeologists to figure out the age of potentially any **organic** object up to around 50,000 years old. This meant bone, cloth, and plant fibers could now be dated. This new technique, pioneered by American chemist Willard Frank Libby in the late 1940s, revolutionized archaeology.

Testing the method

The new method was tested with wood samples from the tombs of two Egyptian pharaohs, Djoser and Sneferu. Historians had previously dated the samples to around 2625 BCE. Using radiocarbon dating, they calculated the age to be 2800 BCE, plus or minus 250 years. The result led to a "radiocarbon revolution" in archaeology. As more objects were tested, many historians were forced to revise their dates and chronologies.

⌄ For his role in developing radiocarbon dating, Willard Libby was awarded the Nobel Prize in Chemistry in 1960.

THE SCIENCE BEHIND: RADIOCARBON DATING

All living things contain carbon. Carbon has more than one type of **atom**. Different atoms of the same element are called **isotopes**. One of the isotopes of carbon is called carbon-14. It is extremely rare: perhaps one in a trillion carbon atoms is carbon-14. But carbon-14 is crucial for dating things because it is **radioactive**. This means it is unstable and decays. Half of the atoms will decay in a precise period of time, known as the half-life. The half-life of carbon-14 is 5,730 years. We can count the number of carbon-14 atoms in a piece of organic material and compare it to the number of carbon-14 atoms in material living today. This helps us figure out how long ago the organism died and, then, the age of the object.

Radiocarbon dating has been used to date some famous **relics**. One was the Turin Shroud, a burial cloth bearing the image of a man who some believe to be Jesus Christ. A sample from the shroud was tested in 1988 and found to date from the 13th or 14th century, many years after Christ. This casts the shroud's **authenticity** into doubt.

⌄ Many believe that the Turin Shroud bears the image of Jesus Christ's body after he was crucified.

Radiocarbon problems

For radiocarbon dating to be accurate, the amount of carbon-14 in the atmosphere needs to be constant throughout history, but this is not the case. Climate change, solar activity, and human activity can affect it. But tree rings reflect these changes. So, archaeologists compare radiocarbon dating results with tree-ring data to get more accurate dates.

Human-made materials

The dating techniques we've learned about so far can only date organic, or natural, materials. In the early 1960s, a new method called thermoluminescence dating was developed by archaeologist Martin Aitken. This could be used to figure out the age of ceramics, such as pottery, bricks, and tiles, that are found buried in the ground.

Testing bricks

Thermoluminescence dating was used to determine the age of the church of Saint-Martin in Angers, France. It was believed to be an 11th-century construction, but testing on the bricks in its bell tower revealed that it was probably built in the 9th century.

THE SCIENCE BEHIND: THERMOLUMINESCENCE DATING

The method is based on the fact that ceramics are crystalline substances. This means their atoms are arranged in an ordered pattern, or **lattice**. There are always imperfections within this lattice. **Electrons** get trapped in these imperfections, causing ceramics to store an electric charge, much like a battery. The charge gradually builds up while the sample is buried underground. The longer it is in the ground, the more energy gets stored (the more the battery is charged). When the sample is heated, it sends out this stored energy as light (luminescence). Scientists heat the ceramic and then measure the amount of light to figure out how old the sample is.

>> The Uffington White Horse is the oldest chalk-cut figure in the United Kingdom. Using optical dating, researchers figured out that the figure was created between 1400 and 600 BCE.

A method known as optical dating, invented in 1984, used a similar principle to thermoluminescence dating to figure out when a mineral was last exposed to daylight. The method was used to date the Nazca lines in the Nazca Desert in Peru. These are human-made arrangements of stones forming giant shapes that are so enormous they can only properly be identified from the air. Optical dating of the mineral quartz buried when the stone lines were constructed indicates that the Nazca lines were made sometime between 100 and 700 CE.

Volcanoes and archaeology

Archaeologists can date sites by examining the traces of ancient volcanic eruptions. When volcanoes erupt, they spew ash over very large areas, and the makeup of this ash is unique to each volcano. So, if an archaeologist finds a layer of volcanic ash at a site, he or she can analyze the ash and compare it to records from previous documented eruptions. That way, the site can be dated. This method is called tephrochronology, because ash layers are known as "tephra."

Using Earth's magnetism

Earth is a giant magnet. You can see this every time you use a compass. The size and direction of Earth's magnetic field (the area that is magnetic) changes over time. Scientists have been able to chart these changes over a span of millions of years. Earth's magnetic field extends far out into space, but it's also inside the planet, and that is what makes it useful to archaeologists.

Sometimes the changes in the magnetic field can get "frozen" inside certain rocks—those containing materials such as iron. This happens when the rocks are heated above a certain temperature. We can tell how old these rocks are by checking their "magnetic signature."

This works for clay, too. When a clay artifact is fired in a kiln, its magnetic signature is fixed permanently within it. This means archaeologists can analyze the clay artifact's age.

Obsidian and prehistory

Obsidian is a hard, dark, glass-like volcanic rock. It can be ground to sharp points and edges and so was used by prehistoric people to make cutting tools and weapons. Obsidian tools are found at prehistoric sites all over the world, from Alaska to the Middle East. Dating obsidian is useful because it can be used to date entire historic sites.

Obsidian absorbs moisture from the atmosphere at a steady rate. This forms a "rind," or a water-rich layer, that increases in depth over time. By measuring the rind's depth, an archaeologist can date the object.

Dating climate changes

Sometimes water itself, in the form of ice, can give us clues about historical climate change. The ice sheets that cover our polar regions (the Arctic and Antarctica) contain within them a detailed record of Earth's climate going back hundreds of thousands of years. Using a special hollow drill, scientists remove tube-shaped samples, known as **ice cores**, from the ice sheet for analysis.

The ice contains evidence of climate changes and major events. For example, volcanic eruptions and forest fires leave traces of ash in the ice. Expanding deserts or high winds leave increased amounts of dust.

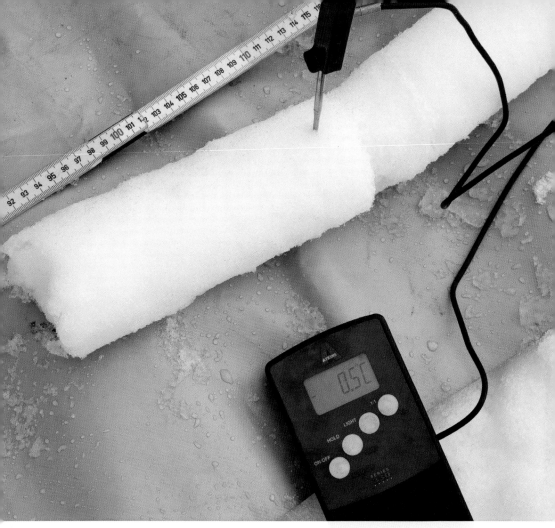

∧ Analyzing the air contained in bubbles trapped in the ice reveals variations in carbon dioxide levels.

CASE STUDY / ROMAN POLLUTION

A study of ice-core samples from Greenland has shown that there was an increase in methane, a potentially polluting gas, starting around 100 BCE. The researchers concluded that this must have been caused by the growth in Roman **agriculture** and metalworking around this time. How do they know this? Livestock, such as cows and sheep, produce methane. Blacksmiths (metalworkers) can also produce methane when they make metal tools and weapons.

4 EXAMINING BODIES

The study of human remains can reveal a lot about how people lived in the past. These studies can tell us about:

- their diet
- their lifestyle
- their diseases
- how they died.

Most human remains consist of bones and teeth, but sometimes entire mummified bodies are discovered. These are bodies that have been preserved, either deliberately or accidentally, through exposure to chemicals, extreme cold, very dry conditions, or lack of air.

The naked tooth

Dental enamel, the white, glossy substance that covers teeth, is the hardest material in the human body. This means teeth are often preserved when bones are not. Teeth contain lots of information, which can be studied with technology. For example, tiny scratches on tooth enamel, visible under a microscope, give clues about a person's diet.

⌄ This ancient human tooth, discovered at an archaeological site near Rosh Haain in Israel, is about 400,000 years old.

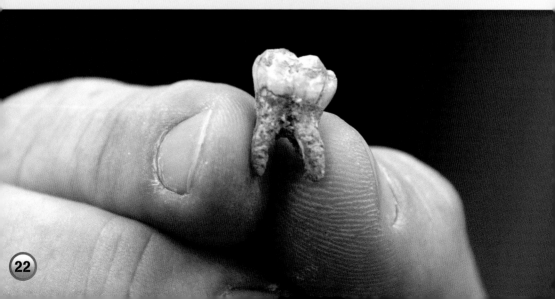

Teeth go through stages of change and loss over a lifetime, so studying teeth can tell us all about a person. Teeth found in a 3,200-year-old tomb in Khirbet Nisya, Israel, gave many clues about people buried there. The wear on the teeth was typical of wheat and barley eaters who had little meat in their diet. Many of the teeth found were from young people. A quarter of the population did not reach age 10, and almost half died before they were 40.

History from hair

Hair can also be tested to determine the age, diet, and health of people. One study of the hair of Peruvians living between 550 and 1532 CE found that they suffered from stress.

Researchers tested hair samples in a process that separated out different chemical substances contained within the hair. A hormone called cortisol, which the body produces when under stress, was discovered in large quantities in the hair samples. The Peruvians could have felt stress because of a lack of food or drought conditions.

TECHNOLOGY THROUGH TIME: STUDYING HUMAN REMAINS

Until the second half of the 20th century, the information from human remains was fairly limited. Specialists could examine bones and figure out the age and sex of an individual. They could study teeth and get clues about diet. They could examine skeletons to learn about deformities or injuries to bones.

A detailed understanding of ancient people's lifestyle, geographical origins, nutrition, health, diseases, ancestry, and appearance became possible thanks to several technological breakthroughs. These are mentioned elsewhere in this book and include:

- computed tomography—late 1960s
- stable isotope analysis—1970s
- **DNA** testing—1980s
- computerized facial reconstruction—from the mid-1980s.

What can isotopes teach us?

In the 1970s, a new technique of studying human remains was developed called stable isotope analysis. Isotopes are different forms of an element (see page 17). Some stay the same (are stable), while others decay and eventually disappear (are unstable).

Isotopes of carbon, calcium, and oxygen are absorbed by living things, including humans, every day. By examining stable isotopes in human remains, archaeologists can see how people lived in the past.

Ancient people on the move

Oxygen and strontium isotopes are useful for figuring out how ancient peoples moved from place to place. This is because the parts of the human body where these isotopes collect—tooth enamel (see pages 22–23) and bone—are formed at different stages of a person's life. Tooth enamel forms early on and doesn't change much with age. This means the strontium or oxygen isotopes in enamel will match those of other items found in the area where people spent their childhood. Bone changes over a lifetime, so it shows where ancient peoples spent the last part of their lives.

CASE STUDY

ANALYZING ROYAL BONES

King Yax K'uk Mo was a king of the Maya, a civilization that flourished in Central America from 250 to 900 CE. Some archaeologists believed he originally came from hundreds of miles away from the Mayan city of Copán. However, stable isotope analysis of the king's bones revealed that he had been born much closer to Copán, possibly in the jungles of northern Guatemala. This raises questions about population movement in Mayan times.

Ancient diets

We absorb carbon and nitrogen isotopes when we eat. By studying the amounts of carbon and nitrogen isotopes in people's remains, scientists can see whether they mainly ate meat, fish, or vegetables. This can also help us to build up a picture of how these societies were organized, based on who ate the most precious type of food.

J. C. VOGEL AND N. J. VAN DER MERWE

Stable isotope analysis was developed in the 1970s by archaeologists J. C. Vogel and N. J. van der Merwe. They published their first study using this method in 1977. It described their analysis of human ribs found at archaeological sites in New York dating from around 2500 BCE to 1300 CE. By studying the amounts of different kinds of isotopes in the ribs from the different sites, they were able to show that the earliest peoples in this area did not eat maize (corn); only later had it become a part of their diet.

⌄ This machine examines the isotope signatures in human remains. These can give clues about how people lived, ate, and moved around in the past.

Ancient DNA

In the 1980s, a powerful tool became available to archaeologists: DNA testing. DNA is a **molecule** found in the cells of all living creatures. It's the major part of **genes**, which determine an organism's physical **characteristics**.

Sequencing DNA

After taking DNA from human remains, such as bones, teeth, and even **feces**, scientists sequence it. In other words, they figure out the order in which the nucleotides (the units that make up the DNA) are arranged within the sample. Archaeologists can analyze this sequence to learn things such as the sex of individuals and how people were related to one another.

Two types of DNA

Our cells contain two types of DNA: mitochondrial (which we **inherit** from our mothers) and nuclear (which we inherit from both parents). We have much more mitochondrial DNA (mtDNA) than nuclear DNA (nDNA). After we die, nDNA breaks down at least twice as fast as mtDNA. Therefore, most of the DNA archaeologists manage to extract from human remains is mtDNA. This offers less information than nDNA, but it is useful for finding family connections between people through the female line.

TECHNOLOGY THROUGH TIME: ANCIENT DNA

1983: Kary Mullis develops PCR (polymerase chain reaction), a way of **amplifying** a single piece of DNA, creating thousands or millions of copies. This greatly speeds up the process of sequencing DNA.

1984: The study of ancient DNA testing begins when Russell Higuchi, a researcher at the University of California, Berkeley, extracts and sequences DNA from a museum specimen of a quagga, an extinct species of zebra.

1985: Biologist Svante Pääbo follows this up by doing the same with mummified human samples.

1997: A team led by Pääbo extracts DNA from a Neanderthal (extinct species of human) fossil that is between 30,000 and 100,000 years old.

2013: DNA is extracted from a 400,000-year-old human thigh bone.

Mummies

The best source of ancient DNA comes from mummified remains. These might be:

- natural mummies preserved in ice, such as Ötzi the Ice Man (see page 29)
- natural mummies that were rapidly dried due to the climate in which they were left, such as those found in the Andes Mountains in South America
- artificial mummies preserved in chemicals, such as the mummies of ancient Egypt.

CASE STUDY / TUTANKHAMUN

In 2010, researchers analyzed DNA from the ancient Egyptian boy-king Tutankhamun (who reigned 1332–1323 BCE) and some of his relatives. They could only extract tiny amounts of DNA because the preserving chemicals used by the ancient Egyptians damaged the bodies' cells, but they managed to amplify these using PCR (see the box on page 26). The results revealed that Tutankhamun's parents may have been brother and sister, and that he may have died from the infectious disease malaria.

⌃ The mummy of Tutankhamun was discovered in 1922. Now, through DNA testing, we are learning more about how he lived and died.

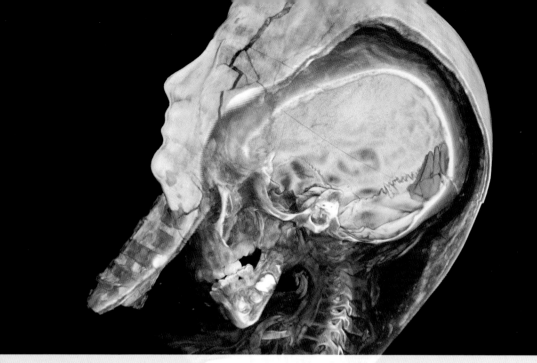

⌃ This is a CT scan of an Egyptian child mummy. These views can teach us a great deal about the health and injuries of ancient Egyptians.

What lies beneath?

The discovery of X-rays in 1895 helped people, for the first time, to look beneath the surface of things without damaging them. This was useful for archaeologists who wanted to know more about their discoveries. By 1898, **Egyptologist** William Flinders Petrie was performing X-rays on Egyptian mummies to examine the body beneath the bandages.

Since then, hundreds of mummies have been X-rayed, sometimes with unexpected results. In several cases, more than one body, or an extra head or leg, has been found inside a wrapped mummy.

Three dimensions

X-rays pass straight through the body's soft tissues, such as muscles and skin. This is why those tissues don't show up on X-ray pictures.

In the early 1970s, 2-D computed tomography (CT) scanners were developed. These used X-rays and a computer to show detailed images of the inside of the body, such as of organs and soft tissues. 3-D versions of these scanners emerged in the 2000s. These give a sense of the depth and internal structure of bodies.

In 2014, eight Egyptian mummies were CT-scanned, giving remarkable insights into their lives and deaths. One man from Thebes, who died around 600 BCE, was found to have dental **abscesses**. These would have been very painful and may have been a cause of death if the infection had gotten into his bloodstream. The scans also showed that the person who preserved the body left part of the metal tool he was using to remove the man's brain inside the skull!

CASE STUDY / ÖTZI THE ICE MAN

The most famous mummy of recent times is Ötzi the Ice Man, who was discovered by German hikers in the Austrian Alps in September 1991. Various tests were done on Ötzi.

- Radiocarbon dating revealed that he lived about 3300 BCE, making him Europe's oldest naturally formed mummy.

- Stable isotope analysis of his tooth enamel and pollen on his clothing showed that he spent his childhood near the modern village of Feldthurns, and later went to live in valleys 30 miles (50 kilometers) further north.

- CT scans of his stomach and intestines showed that he'd eaten meals of red deer, herb bread, grain, roots, and fruits. Scans also revealed an arrowhead lodged in his shoulder and several cracked ribs.

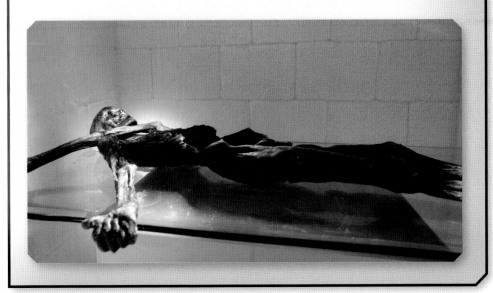

Re-creating faces

Skeletal remains can't tell us much by themselves about what our ancestors actually looked like. But thanks to advances in computing and imaging technology, it's now becoming possible to reconstruct faces using skulls. This may be the closest we will ever get to seeing the faces of people who lived thousands of years ago. However, it is a technique that has some potential problems.

CASE STUDY / RICHARD III

England's King Richard III was killed at the Battle of Bosworth, England, in 1485. In 2012, his skeleton was discovered underneath a parking lot in Leicester, England. After doing DNA and radiocarbon dating tests to prove it was the king, a team from the University of Dundee set about creating a facial reconstruction based on the skull. They wanted to provide further evidence that this was indeed King Richard. The team didn't look at any portraits of the king while creating the model, to avoid being influenced by them.

1. A 3-D scan was made of the skull.

2. The computer added layers of muscle and skin.

3. The computer scan was reproduced as a 3-D plastic model.

4. **Prosthetic** eyes were added, along with a wig, hat, and clothing.

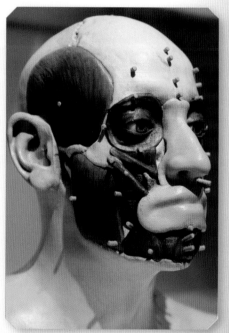

⌃ The reconstructed face of King Richard has a slightly arched nose and prominent chin, similar to features shown in portraits of the king. Of course, this is an approximation of what Richard may have looked like. Some historians have said there is not enough evidence to create people's faces entirely.

Computer modeling

In the 2000s, computerized techniques for 3-D facial reconstruction were becoming more sophisticated. In 2003, sculptor Christian Corbet created a facial reconstruction of a 2,200-year-old mummy based on CT and laser scans—the first of its kind.

The skull is first captured in digital form by a 3-D laser scanner. Computer programs then transform the image into a face and head, building it up in layers in the same way as clay modeling. Computer modelers sometimes make CT scans of the heads of living people in order to get an accurate measurement of tissue depth.

Computerized images can be produced more quickly than clay models, and it is easier to make adjustments. The image can then be given a physical form by printing it out on a 3-D printer.

THE SCIENCE BEHIND: CLAY MODELING

Archaeologists and anthropologists (people who study human history) have long been interested in reconstructing ancient faces, and attempts to do so were made as far back as the 1880s. Facial reconstructions were made using modeling clay as follows:

1. Clean the skull and repair any damaged areas with wax.
2. Reattach the lower jaw, fill the nostrils, and place artificial eyes in the eye sockets.
3. Prepare a plaster cast of the skull.
4. Attach matchsticks to the cast to show the average thickness of facial tissue.
5. Add features with modeling clay in the following order: facial muscles; nose and lips; muscles of facial expression; soft tissue around the eyes; and ears.
6. Flesh out the face with clay until the matchsticks are covered.
7. Apply hair, coloring, wrinkles, and other features.

5 EXAMINING ARTIFACTS

Every item that archaeologists recover from the ground is potentially really exciting. Whether it is a work of art or a simple spoon, it could add a lot of knowledge about past cultures.

Studying artifacts helps us understand how past societies worked. They can teach us what ancient people felt about things like family, religion, and the world around them. In recent years, technological advances have allowed archaeologists to learn even more about the artifacts they dig up.

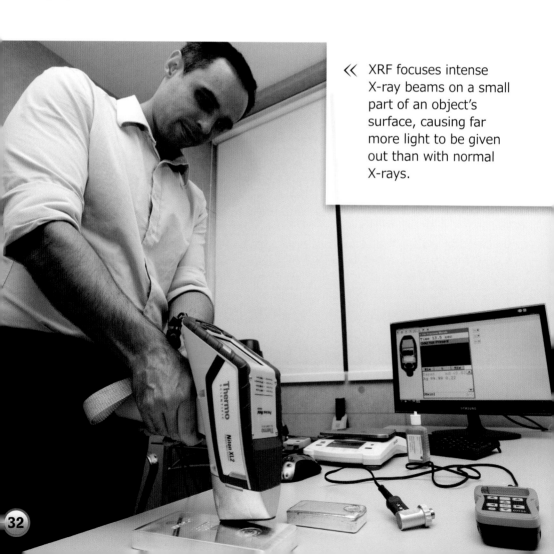

« XRF focuses intense X-ray beams on a small part of an object's surface, causing far more light to be given out than with normal X-rays.

ROBERT THORNE

In 2005, archaeologists used XRF to read an inscription (words cut into the surface) on a piece of Roman pottery. Robert Thorne and his team found minute traces of pigment (color) on the pottery surface, as well as iron from the chisel that made the inscription. From this, they were able to identify a crucial letter. The same team later applied XRF to the inscriptions and decorations on some badly worn Mayan pottery.

What is it made of?

X-rays can also reveal what chemicals things are made of. When an object is X-rayed, the ray's energy "excites" the atoms within it. If the energy is great enough, the atoms can lose an electron, a process that causes them to give out light.

A process called X-ray fluorescence (XRF) is especially useful. It analyzes light to figure out what kind of atoms are contained within the material.

Separating substances

If you place blotting paper in a pool of ink, you may notice the ink defying gravity and climbing up the paper. This is a property of liquid called capillary action. The ink separates into a clear area, which climbs through the paper, and a dark area, which lags behind.

This is the basis of a process called chromatography. It relies on each ingredient of the ink reacting differently to the paper. It's useful for scientists who wish to analyze the individual parts of a liquid or a gas.

"Chromatography" is a general term for a family of techniques that involve separating mixtures. The most powerful of these is gas chromatography (GC). Archaeologists use GC to separate the ingredients of a substance in a glass column.

In this glass column, a device called a **mass spectrometer** (MS) is used to identify ingredients. This allows them to identify substances found at historical sites, such as charred food remains in pottery containers.

Chemical fingerprints

Archaeologists don't only want to know what an artifact is made of—they're also interested in finding out where its material originally came from and about the **microstructure** of the item itself. **Neutron** activation analysis (NAA) allows them to find out where it comes from (see the box, right), whereas using a scanning electron microscope (SEM) can magnify the item (see below).

Looking up close

Sometimes it's useful to view an artifact in minute detail. This can be done with an instrument called a scanning electron microscope (SEM), which can magnify objects by up to 300,000 times. The SEM also gives much greater depth than an ordinary microscope. It produces detailed 3-D images in which every groove and engraving stands out.

THE SCIENCE BEHIND: THE SCANNING ELECTRON MICROSCOPE

Unlike ordinary "light" microscopes, which use lenses to magnify an object, the SEM uses electrons. At the top of the SEM is an "electron gun," which fires a beam of electrons at a sample. The beam slowly moves back and forth across the sample's surface, interacting with the atoms there, dislodging their electrons. The SEM attracts these scattered electrons, which it records as different levels of brightness on a monitor.

SEM's level of magnification can tell us a lot about how artifacts were made. For example, by using an SEM to analyze the microstructure of **medieval** bricks from Switzerland, archaeologists were able to figure out how hot the kiln used to fire the clay was! And in a study of chert (a type of rock) blades in the Indus Valley, SEM images showed traces of the copper tool that was used to make them.

A Roman mystery
The origins of a bronze statuette of the Roman goddess Minerva, held at the British Museum in London, seemed destined to remain a mystery—until SEM analysis of the object uncovered an important clue.

Minute black crystals were found embedded in the bronze, and these could only have come from one place and time: Pompeii, Italy, in 79 CE. That was the year when the volcano Vesuvius erupted, engulfing the Roman city. The crystals in the statuette were identical to those found in other objects buried in Pompeii's ashes.

⌄ Dot by dot, row by row, the SEM forms an incredibly detailed image of a sample.

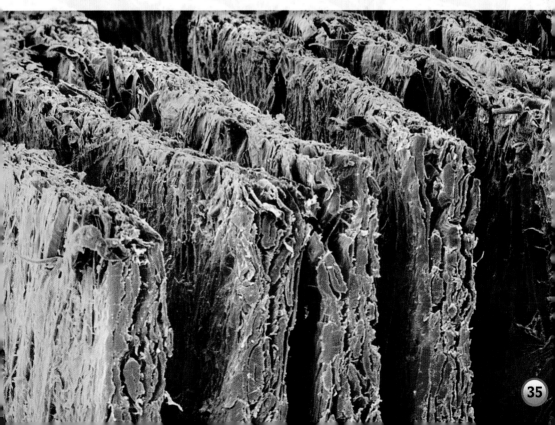

Studying surfaces

Sometimes it is the surface of an object that archaeologists find interesting. Maybe they want to know how ancient people made the colors that decorate their pottery, or they want to find out what ingredients made the ink on an old document. This is possible using a technique called Raman spectroscopy.

THE SCIENCE BEHIND: RAMAN SPECTROSCOPY

This method works by shining a laser beam onto the surface of an object. Some of this laser light interacts with molecules in the material and is scattered (known as the Raman effect). The scattered light forms a pattern, which acts as a fingerprint to identify the surface materials.

⌄ Raman spectroscopy has been used to analyze prehistoric cave art, including drawings of mammoths, dating from 13,500 to 12,000 years ago in Rouffignac, France.

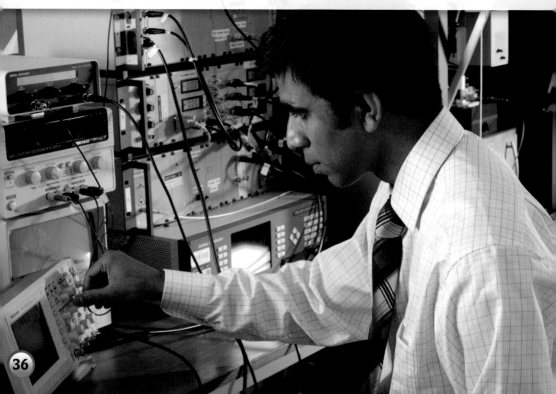

CASE STUDY — THE VINLAND MAP

The Vinland Map is a map of North America, which appears to show that Europeans settled there before Columbus's arrival in 1492. In 2002, Raman spectroscopy was used to analyze the map's ink to check the claim that the map dates from the 15th century. The ink was black with an underlying yellowish layer, common in 15th-century ink. But the black ink was found to be carbon based, so should not have left a yellow stain. The yellow layer was identified as yellow anatase, which only became available in 1917. Researchers concluded that the Vinland Map was made in the 20th century and made to look old by the use of yellow anatase to mimic medieval ink.

Looking without damaging

Archaeologists want to avoid damaging artifacts. But bombarding objects with X-rays or **subatomic particles** causes damage, especially if they are fragile. Yet if we can't use these methods, much of the history of these relics will remain locked away.

One way around this problem is to use smaller samples. Lasers make this possible. They can produce a focused and intense beam of light, so that only a very small area of an artifact is needed for analysis.

Lasers with a light touch

Laser-induced breakdown spectroscopy (LIBS) uses a laser pulse to "excite" a tiny amount of material. The amount affected can be measured in nanograms, or billionths of a gram, which is why LIBS causes very little damage to artifacts.

The material is heated to extremely high temperatures—over 180,000 degrees Fahrenheit (100,000 degrees Celsius). The heat is enough to remove particles from the sample's surface to form a plume of plasma—a gas made of excited atoms. These give out light, which the archaeologist then analyzes with a spectrometer (see page 33).

LIBS has many advantages:
* The equipment is portable.
* The process can be carried out in the field, rather than in the laboratory.
* It provides results almost immediately.

6 HISTORY IN THE COMPUTER AGE

So far in this book, we have looked at the impact of technology on archaeology. But technology has also influenced the way history is studied. History is the study of humans in the past since the invention of writing. Since the early 1990s, the main technological advances that have affected history have been computing and the Internet.

Advantages of the Internet

Thanks to the Internet, we are all now much more connected, with instant access to information, research, and primary sources. This has many advantages for historians, for example:

- Today, a historian's research can be viewed by people all around the world. If you want to find something out, it's just a few clicks away.
- Historians can **collaborate** on research, no matter how far apart they live. They can learn about new historical or archaeological discoveries almost as soon as they are made.

In 2011, the Getty Research Institute created a collaborative research project. It uploaded a 17th-century manuscript to its web site—a list of paintings written in the form of rhyming poetry. They invited art historians from all over the world to help figure out which paintings were being referred to.

Today, anybody can do their own historical projects with access to the Internet. History is not simply the study of great nations and empires—it's also about ordinary people and how they lived. The Internet has made it easier for those kinds of stories to be told. For more on this topic, see pages 46–47.

Disadvantages of the Internet

Professional historians are trained in how to assess evidence and put forward a balanced, reasoned argument. Their books and articles are peer-reviewed (checked by fellow professionals) before being published. This is why we can be reasonably confident about the facts we find in history books and journals.

By contrast, the open nature of the Internet means that there are no controls or checks on what is put out there. Anyone can post, and their articles aren't necessarily accurate. Distorted views of historical events can be read by anyone, and that is why it is important to always use **authoritative** sites. These can be web sites belonging to museums, reference publishers, reputable encyclopedias, and world-renowned institutions, such as the Smithsonian.

TECHNOLOGY THROUGH TIME: HISTORICAL RESEARCH

Traditionally, historians relied on visits to libraries and **archives** to do their research and use primary source material. In the 1960s, some historians started using computers to help them process data from historical records. The biggest change, however, came in the early 1990s with the arrival of the World Wide Web. Historical archives were **digitized** and placed online, making it much easier to access them for research. Historians also now work closer with scientists than ever before.

Digital history

Since the dawn of the Internet, a number of universities have established departments specifically for the development of "digital history" projects. These include the Roy Rosenzweig Center for History and New Media (RRCHNM) at George Mason University, in Fairfax, Virginia, and the University of Virginia's Virginia Center for Digital History, in Charlottesville, Virginia.

Topics for digital history projects have included the French Revolution, migration, and the slave trade. The projects are made up of analysis of historical documents and images. What makes them different from other web sites is that they include digital tools to enhance that analysis. Another one of these projects is the SIMILE project, discussed in the box below.

PIONEERS

A NEW KIND OF TIMELINE

The SIMILE project, created by the Massachusetts Institute of Technology, in Cambridge, Massachusetts, develops tools to help users access and make use of digital collections, including history projects. One of these tools is an app that allows users to create their own interactive timelines to help visualize events as they unfolded. Users can scroll along the timeline with their mouse and click on items to link to more information and images.

Searchable text

Digital history also makes it much easier for historians to search through thousands of documents, thanks to searchable text.

One example is a project called Valley of the Shadow. This focuses on U.S. society during and after the Civil War. All of the archive's letters, diaries, and newspaper articles have been digitized to allow users to search the text for keywords, names, and dates.

ARCHAEOLOGY GREECE EVENT MAYAN EVIDENCE AGES WESTERN AZTEC POLITICAL FIRST SOURCE SECONDARY CIVILIZATION BYZANTINE IMPORTANT ROME LIFE **HISTORY** PRIMARY HISTORIAN ANCIENT EGYPT ANGLO-SAXON

∧ Word clouds tell us about how language is used.

One piece of software, developed at the University of Nebraska's Center for Digital Research in the Humanities, in Lincoln, Nebraska, creates lists that show how frequently words are used. It can present these as "word clouds"—a visual way to show how often words crop up, with the most commonly used words shown largest. This can help reveal the way language is used in historical documents.

Mapping the data

One other tool to enhance analysis of information is Geographic Information Systems (GIS). This is a computer system designed to capture, store, analyze, and display all types of geographical information. GIS can show many types of data on one map, making it easier for people to see and understand patterns and relationships.

CASE STUDY / SLAVERY PROJECT

GIS was used in a digital history project called The Differences Slavery Made, which looked at how slavery divided U.S. society, focusing on two communities (Franklin, Pennsylvania, and Augusta, Virginia). The project contained GIS maps of the communities that included roads, streams, railroads, footpaths, and even individual houses and farms, with information on the type of household, political and religious beliefs, number of slaves, and more, all researched from local records. This approach can help historians visualize in map form the relationships and conflicts described in written sources.

Genetic history

Today, a powerful new research tool has become available to historians: genetics. This is the study of our ancestry through our DNA (see also pages 26–27). The DNA within our cells contains information about our ancestors. These take the form of genetic markers—particular genes, or DNA sequences, that place us within one of the populations that make up the human family.

⋀ The Saami of Scandinavia speak a completely different kind of language from other Europeans, suggesting a different ancestry.

Thanks to advancing computer power, sequencing DNA has become a much quicker process. It is now possible to study the genomes (complete DNA sequences) of large groups of people. This has given us an insight into the origins and movements of groups of people.

PIONEERS

TRACING THE ORIGINS OF THE JAPANESE

Some people think that the earliest signs of human settlement in Japan date from up to 40,000 years ago. Then, in around 11,000 BCE, a culture we call the Jōmon emerged, known mainly from its pottery and other archaeological remains. But where did the Jōmon people come from?

Geneticist Michael Hammer of the University of Arizona searched for a match in other Asian populations. The closest to the Jōmon were the Tibetans, who live about 2,500 miles away. But how could an isolated mountain people thousands of miles to the west have ended up settling Japan? It may be that both are descended from a common Central Asian people, now vanished from the genetic record. Another theory is that Tibetan settlers crossed to Japan on an ice bridge 12,000 to 20,000 years ago. We just don't know.

Matching populations

Researchers test a sample of around 1,500 individuals from a single population and search for **genetic** markers. They then look for other populations that have the same markers and see if they can find a match. For example, we know that in the 13th century, the Mongol Empire under Genghis Khan expanded into the territory of modern-day Pakistan. So, it is not surprising that we can find traces of Mongol DNA in the Hazara people of that region.

Sometimes, however, genetic history offers surprises. For instance, traces of European DNA have been found in the Tu people of China. How did it get there? Perhaps European merchants mixed with the Tu while traveling the Silk Road. This was the trade route linking Europe to Asia during ancient and medieval times.

Genetic history has helped to establish where European people came from. In a 2013 study, DNA was analyzed from 364 skeletons in Germany. This DNA indicated that modern-day Europeans may have been descended from farmers who moved northwest from Anatolia (modern Turkey) to central Europe around 7,000 years ago.

⌄ DNA analysis has revealed the origins of the Tu people in China.

Virtual heritage

Today, technology allows archaeologists, historians, and members of the public access to historic sites without having to actually visit them. But it wasn't always like this.

Virtual heritage at Nimrud

Virtual heritage (VH) is a revolution in archaeology and history studies. It uses tools such as 3-D modeling, graphics, animation, and virtual reality to re-create sites as they might have appeared when they were in use. One good example of its use is in present-day Iraq, at Nimrud.

Assyrian king Ashurnasirpal II built his spectacular North-West Palace at Nimrud in the 9th century BCE. Today, its wall reliefs (carvings on a wall) and artifacts are scattered among more than 80 museums and private collections, and the palace itself is under threat from pollution, looting, and an unsettled political situation. A VH project was set up to reassemble its many treasures in one virtual site and to test out theories about how the building was used.

To re-create the palace, the project's creators spent a lot of time at the site checking the topography (arrangement of physical features) and major monuments. They then read old excavation reports and looked at photographs and drawings of the surviving reliefs. This process, and the completed model, gave them new insights into how the Assyrians may have used the spaces within the palace. They also discovered mistakes in previous archaeologists' drawings of the space.

CASE STUDY / THE TANTURA SHIPWRECKS

Some sites benefit from VH because they are too difficult or expensive to reach or too fragile to allow public access. This is the case with an underwater site at Tantura Lagoon off the coast of Israel, where the wrecks of a number of 9th- and 10th-century Arab trading ships lie in shallow water.

The producers of the VH project took hundreds of high-resolution color photos, which they used to create 3-D reconstructions of the site. They wanted users to imagine themselves diving among the wrecks and exploring the site up close.

TECHNOLOGY THROUGH TIME: ARCHAEOLOGY ON DISPLAY

pre-1840s: Archaeologists present their work as text and drawings.

1840s: Archaeologists begin using cameras to record and distribute images of the artifacts they dig up.

1890s: Archaeologists start taking photographs of archaeological sites, to document and study the sites without being there.

1950s: British archaeologist Mortimer Wheeler and his photographer Maurice Cookson are the first to use photography to demonstrate methods of excavation, turning the camera into a scientific tool.

1993: Launch of the first VH project—a 12th Dynasty Egyptian fortress called Buhen is brought back to life as a 3-D computer re-creation, heralding the arrival of a powerful new medium for displaying historic sites.

This model in the Israel Museum, Jerusalem, shows how the city of Jerusalem looked around 2,000 years ago. Scale models of ancient cities and archaeological sites are an effective way to bring history to life.

7 THE FUTURE

How might technology benefit historians and archaeologists in the future? We can already see trends developing. Internet access will grow, further opening history to the public. In archaeology, the physical work of excavation will probably continue, but new methods may emerge for finding sites and analyzing what is found there.

Anyone can be a historian

Thanks to the Internet, anyone can research, create, and publish their own digital history project. This could be anything from the story of their hometown to photos commemorating a famous event. Amateur historians can use social media to invite others to send their own pictures and stories. This is called **crowdsourcing**, and it is transforming the way history is studied.

In the United States, Make History records the events of the 9/11 attacks through the eyes of those who experienced them. It includes photos, videos, voice messages, and memorabilia connected to the day.

Hundreds of crowdsourced history projects are being created all over the world. For example, the Kigali Genocide Memorial Center in Rwanda has created a project that aims to record the experiences of survivors of the 1994 Rwanda genocide.

CASE STUDY / NATIONAL ARCHIVES AND RECORDS ADMINISTRATION

In 2012, the U.S. National Archives and Records Administration (NARA) asked the public to help tag and caption its collection. The archive contains 8 billion historical documents, of which only a small fraction have been cataloged. They include such items as letters from presidents and Civil War casualty lists. Every day, researchers, including members of the public, are uncovering material that no one knew existed, much of which could be helpful to historians.

Digital volunteers

Ordinary citizens are not only able to record their own histories, but they can also become "digital volunteers" and help catalog a nation's archives. So far, U.S. institutions are in the forefront of this drive to recruit citizen archivists. Their success suggests that the trend will continue and will certainly spread to other countries.

ᐱ In Germany, a project called "We Were So Free" is building an archive of people's memories of the fall of the Berlin Wall (1989) and German reunification (1990).

PIONEERS

HARNESSING THE POWER OF CROWDS

The Library of Congress had a problem. About half of its collection of around 12 million historical photos was of little use to researchers because the photos were not properly captioned. In 2007, the library published several thousand photographs on the photo-sharing web site Flickr and asked the public for help in identifying them. Amateurs set to work on topics ranging from World War II bomber planes to early 20th-century boxing, and they identified a remarkable number of photographs.

The future in 3-D

The archaeologists of the future will be armed with more hi-tech tools than shovels and brushes. 3-D imaging will help to uncover sites in ways that photographs cannot. Using software such as Geographical Information Systems (see page 41), archaeologists will be able to create 3-D maps and films of a site. They can also create better quality images of things than ever before.

THE SCIENCE BEHIND: REFLECTANCE TRANSFORMATION IMAGING

Reflectance Transformation Imaging (RTI) is a super hi-resolution technique for scanning pottery. It enhances the surface shape and color of an object and can relight it from any angle, making it even clearer than it would appear under a microscope. How does it work? RTI images are created from multiple digital photos shot with light projected from different directions. A computer converts this information into a 3-D mathematical model of the surface. In the future, RTI is certain to improve. Images will become sharper and brighter, making it easier to analyze surfaces and read ancient inscriptions.

Making maps with drones

Maps can be created faster and more precisely thanks to small, remote-controlled aircraft called drones. These drones fly over a site, recording it with onboard cameras. Because the drones skim so close to the ground,

⌃ This drone has four separate rotors to hover and move through the air for up to 30 minutes. It can even avoid other airborne objects.

they can measure the site with great accuracy. Drones can even be fitted with thermal (heat-sensing) cameras to reveal structures hidden beneath the ground. Currently, drones can fly for a maximum of 15 minutes. However, this is bound to increase because, potentially, drones are very cheap—at least, they are a lot cheaper to operate than piloted aircraft.

The power of technology

Technology is helping historians and archaeologists solve age-old mysteries and unlock the secrets of the past. The latest surveying techniques have helped uncover new sites for excavation, and we have learned to date objects by the effects on them of water and sunlight, or by counting the carbon isotopes they contain.

Stable isotope analysis and DNA testing have revealed much about the lifestyles and migrations of our ancestors. Modern scanning techniques allow us to look inside mummies without damaging them, and computer modeling has helped us to reconstruct the faces of the dead.

Also, we can separate out ancient substances for analysis with chromatography. We can bombard artifacts with particles to reveal their chemical structure. And, thanks to the Internet, historians and ordinary citizens can collaborate as never before in researching history and creating digital archives.

There is no question that technology has changed the way we look at and think about the past. Yet no matter how sophisticated the tools become, we will always need creative and curious people to pose questions that technology cannot yet answer.

TIMELINE

1890s: Archaeologists start to use stratigraphy for relative dating of artifacts

1893: Augustus Pitt-Rivers hammers on the ground with a pick to identify a buried ditch from the variation of sound. It is the first recorded use of a geophysical technique in archaeology.

1898: William Flinders Petrie uses X-rays to examine Egyptian mummies

1901: Andrew Ellicott Douglass develops the dating method called dendrochronology

1920s: Mortimer Wheeler develops the grid system of excavation. Archaeologists help make aerial photography become a popular tool for looking for potential archaeological sites.

1928: Indian scientist C. V. Raman pioneers Raman spectroscopy

1946: Richard Atkinson is the first archaeologist to use an electrical resistance meter to survey a site

1949: Willard Libby develops radiocarbon dating. Archer John Porter Martin and Anthony T. James start to develop gas chromatography.

1950: X-ray fluorescence spectrometers become commercially available

1954: Danish scientist Willi Dansgaard develops ice-core science as a means of studying past climates

1957: Scientists at the Brookhaven National Laboratory, in Upton, New York, are the first to use neutron activation analysis for archaeological investigation

1958: Martin Aitken is the first archaeologist to use a magnetometer to survey a site

1960: George Bass and Peter Throckmorton develop the rules and procedures for marine archaeology

1960: The possibility of thermoluminescence as a means of dating ceramics is first proposed

1960: Irving Friedman and Robert Smith invent obsidian hydration dating

1962: Laser-induced breakdown spectroscopy is invented

1965: Scanning electron microscopes become commercially available

1971: Van der Merwe and Vogel are the first archaeologists to use stable isotope analysis on human remains

1972: Godfrey Hounsfield and Allan Cormack invent computed tomography (CT) scanning. A test version appeared the year before.

1975: Ground penetrating radar (GPR) is first used at archaeological sites

1984: Russell Higuchi develops DNA testing as an archaeological tool

1984: Optical dating (a means of dating when a mineral was last exposed to daylight) is invented

1985: Remotely operated vehicles (ROVs) are used to explore the wreck of the *Titanic*

1988: Radiocarbon dating is used to test the authenticity of the Turin Shroud

1989: Stereophotography is first used to obtain clear images of undersea shipwrecks

1989: Tim Berners-Lee invents the World Wide Web

1991: Ötzi the Ice Man, a 5,300-year-old naturally formed mummy, is discovered in the Austrian Alps

2003: A computerized technique is developed for 3-D facial reconstruction from a skull

2009: Rehydroxylation dating is invented by scientists at the University of Manchester, in the United Kingdom

2010: The potential of LIDAR as a tool for surveying archaeological sites is first realized, thanks to Arlen and Diane Chase's uncovering of Mayan ruins in Central America

GLOSSARY

abscess swollen, painful area either on or in your body, containing pus

aerial from the air

agriculture work of taking care of animals and growing plants that are used for food, sometimes to sell

amplify in genetics, make multiples of (for example, a DNA sequence)

antenna (plural: antennae), rod, wire, or other device used to transmit or receive radio waves

archive collection of historical documents or records

atom basic unit of a chemical element

authenticity when something is genuine and not a copy or a fake

authoritative trusted to be reliable or accurate

Byzantine civilization that lasted until 1453 CE but had its golden era between the 4th and 5th centuries CE

characteristic particular thing, or quality, of someone or something

collaborate work together with other people on an activity

conduct allows electricity, or some other kind of energy, to flow through it

cremation disposal of a dead body by burning it to ashes

crowdsourcing inviting contributions from the public for a specific project. In the modern era, crowdsourcing is usually done online.

digitize convert something into a digital form, which can then be processed by a computer

DNA type of molecule found in every cell of every living thing. It carries genetic information—the information that determines an organism's characteristics.

Egyptologist someone who studies the history, language, literature, and culture of ancient Egyptians

electron negatively charged particle that orbits the nucleus of an atom

evidence facts that tell us whether something is true

excavation digging up of things from the ground

feces formal or medical word for solid waste released from the body

gene part of a cell that is passed between parent and child

genetic relating to genes, the distinct sequences of DNA that transmit characteristics from one generation to the next

high-resolution greatly detailed

hull bottom and sides of a ship or other sailing vessel

human remains person's body after death

ice core tube of polar ice, extracted from an ice sheet and analyzed in order to draw conclusions about climatic conditions in the past

infrared form of electromagnetic radiation with a wavelength just greater than that of the red end of the visible light spectrum

inherit get something from someone related to you, such as a particular gene

isotope different atoms of the same element

lattice regular, repeated, 3-D arrangement of atoms

magnetic field area around a magnetic material within which the force of magnetism acts

mass spectrometer instrument used to separate isotopes and molecules according to their mass (weight)

Mayan of the Mayans, an ancient civilization that flourished in Central America between 250 and 900 CE

medieval period of European history between 500 CE and 1500 CE

microstructure something constructed from smaller parts, which you can only see through a microscope

molecule group of atoms that are bonded together

neutron particle of neutral charge found in the nucleus of an atom

organic made from living matter

prosthetic artificial (human-made) body part

radar system for tracking objects by sending out pulses of radio waves that are reflected off the object back to the radar

radiation kind of energy that is emitted in the form of rays or waves—for example, heat, light, or sound

radioactive describes a substance that gives off energy in the form of a stream of particles, owing to the decaying of its unstable atoms

relic object recovered from an earlier time; sometimes a religious object

sonar system for detecting objects under water by sending out sound pulses and measuring the length or speed of their return after they are reflected back

subatomic particle one of the smallest things from which something can be made

systematic doing something according to a fixed, ordered plan

FIND OUT MORE

Books

Compoint, Stéphane. *Buried Treasures: Uncovering the Secrets of the Past*. New York: Abrams, 2011.

Harasymiw, Mark. *Be an Archaeologist* (Be a Scientist!). New York: Gareth Stevens, 2015.

Hunter, Nick. *Shipwrecks* (Treasure Hunters). Chicago: Raintree, 2013.

Hyde, Natalie. *Human Fossils* (If Fossils Could Talk). St. Catherine's, Ont.: Crabtree, 2014.

Pohl, John M. D., and Judith Levin. *Tenochtitlan* (Digging for the Past). New York: Oxford, 2007.

Web sites

Use FactHound to find Internet sites related to this book. All of the sites on FactHound have been researched by our staff.

Here's all you do:
Visit *www.facthound.com*
Type in this code: 9781484626399

Places to visit

The American Museum of Natural History, New York City
This famous museum contains a huge variety of archaeological specimens and much more.

The Field Museum, Chicago, Illinois
This popular museum is dedicated to human history and life on Earth and has an enormous collection of objects, including the bones of "Sue" the Tyrannosaurus Rex.

Smithsonian National Museum of Natural History,
Washington, D.C.
This museum is dedicated to the study of the natural world and has an amazing collection of archaeological objects.

Further research

1. Create your own digital archive. It could be about a local news event that has caught your interest, the history of your favorite sports team, or even the history of a building in your neighborhood. Use your local library to do research. Include historical photographs, maps, newspaper clippings, and audio clips of any interviews you have carried out.

2. Research an archaeological project of your choice and write a report on it. Include information on the following: When and how was the site or object discovered? What methods did the archaeologists use to determine its age? What techniques did they use to analyze it? What were their conclusions?

INDEX